ROAD TRIP!

Camping with the Four Vagabonds

THOMAS EDISON, HENRY FORD, HARVEY FIRESTONE, and JOHN BURROUGHS

By **Claudia Friddell** / *Illustrated by* **Jeremy Holmes**

CALKINS CREEK
AN IMPRINT OF
ASTRA BOOKS FOR YOUNG READERS
New York

I LIKE TO GET OUT IN THE WOODS *and* LIVE CLOSE *to* NATURE.
EVERY MAN DOES. IT IS *in* HIS BLOOD.
—THOMAS EDISON, *Famous Travelers*

TO THE WOODS and FIELDS or TO THE HILLTOPS,
THERE to BREATHE THEIR BEAUTY like THE VERY AIR;
TO BE NOT A SPECTATOR OF, but A PARTICIPATOR IN, IT ALL!
—JOHN BURROUGHS, *Our Vacation Days of 1918*

DAY AND NIGHT,
Thomas Edison experimented with ways to make life
better for others.

LIGHT

MUSIC

BATTERY

PHONOGRAPH

ELECTRICITY

Sometimes he forgot to eat, and sometimes he forgot
to sleep. Edison hated schedules and routines.
THAT'S HOW HE WORKED BEST.

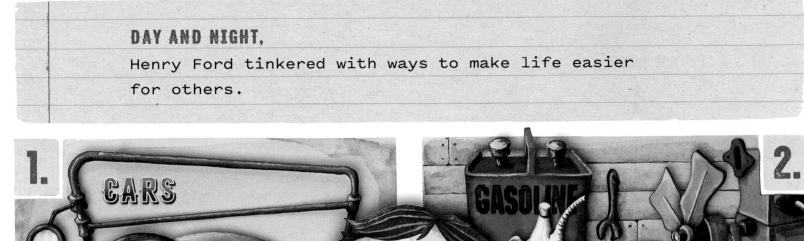

He never forgot to eat, and he never forgot to sleep.
Ford loved schedules and routines.
THAT'S HOW HE WORKED BEST.

After years of making the things that other people needed, the busy friends realized there was something they needed—something that couldn't be made in a laboratory or a factory:

A VACATION!

But where could the famous inventors
who put light into homes and cars on the road
go to escape from their busy lives?

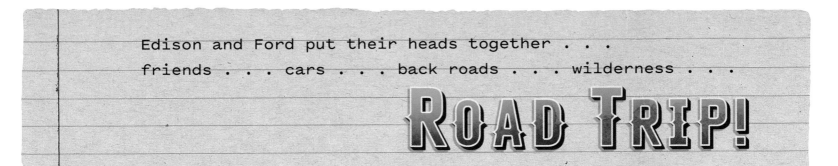

Edison and Ford put their heads together . . .
friends . . . cars . . . back roads . . . wilderness . . .

ROAD TRIP!

In the summer of 1914, Edison invited Ford and his Model T to explore the marshy wilds of the Florida Everglades.

The curious inventors invited along their good
friend John Burroughs. The popular nature writer
not only had a way with words—he had a way with
the great outdoors.

The following summer, Ford and Edison took a road trip down the coast of California with another friend, Harvey Firestone. Firestone was famous for making and selling rubber tires that gave Model Ts a comfortable ride. The tire king not only ran a good company—he *was* good company!

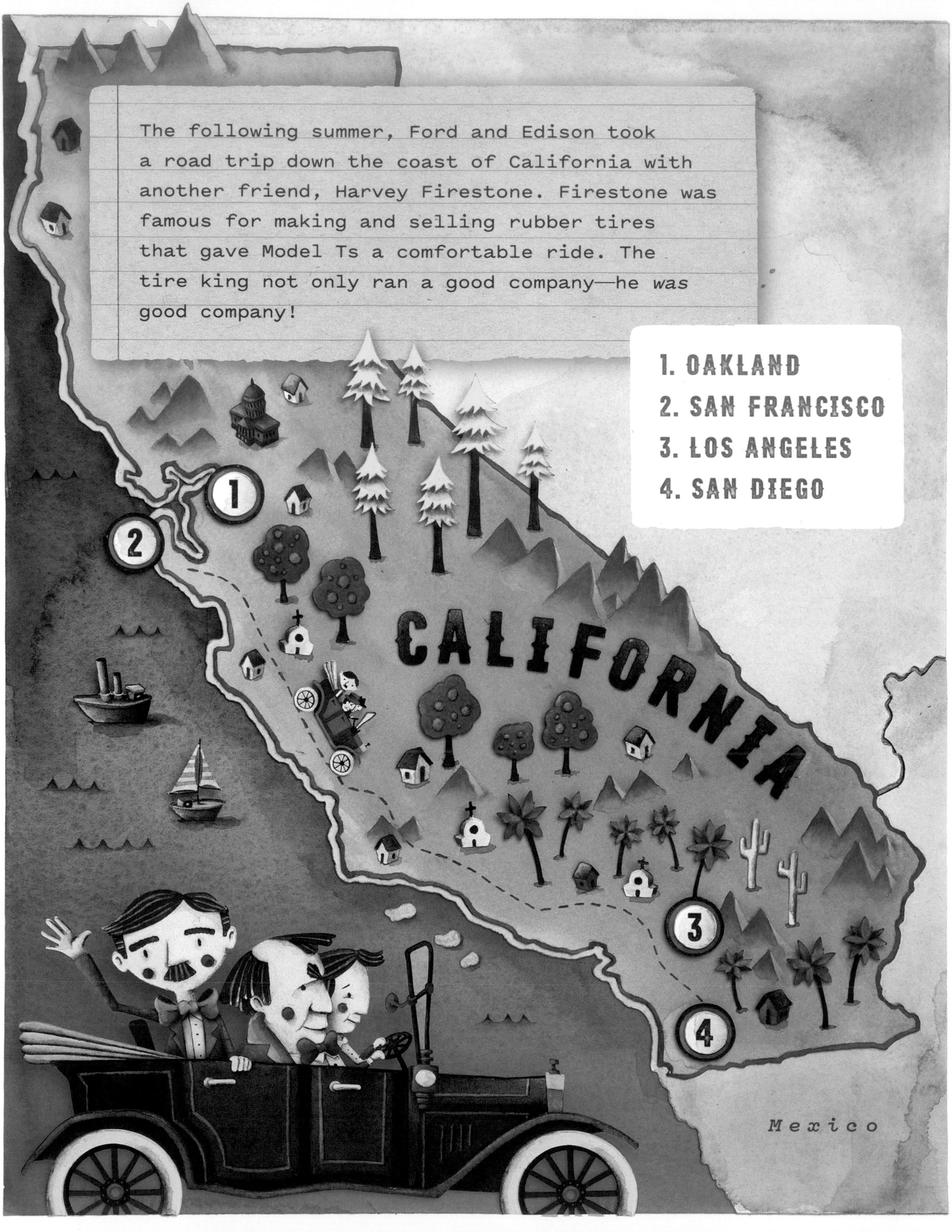

1. OAKLAND
2. SAN FRANCISCO
3. LOS ANGELES
4. SAN DIEGO

CALIFORNIA

Mexico

Having friends like Burroughs and Firestone
reminded the inventors of one of the best ideas
they ever shared:

TEAMWORK!

Edison knew that many bright minds working together in a laboratory were better than just one.

And Ford knew that many strong arms working together on an assembly line were better than just two.

Edison and Ford agreed that their road trips needed all four friends like a car needed all four wheels—but getting all the friends together wasn't so easy.

Finally, in the summer of 1918, the campers
were ready to pack their bags and pick their jobs:

"Captain Tinker"

1. *Activities director
and car mechanic:*
HENRY FORD

"Shall we discuss
our intended Route?"

MAP OF APPALACHIAN TRAIL

2. *Navigator and
discussion leader:*
THOMAS EDISON

"The Chatty Cartographer"

3. *Supply manager and organizer:* HARVEY FIRESTONE

"THE PLAN MAN"

4. *Nature guide and journal writer:* JOHN BURROUGHS

"NATURE'S KNOW-IT-ALL"

The famous friends became the **FOUR VAGABONDS** as they wandered through the Appalachians and the Alleghenies— each night a new campsite, each day a new adventure.

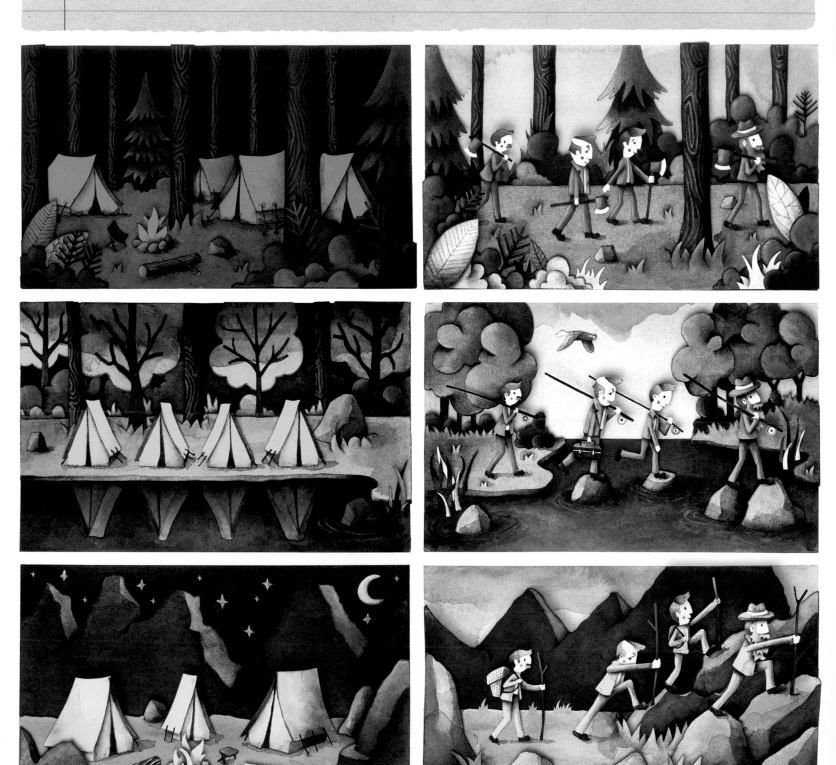

From Pennsylvania to West Virginia, from Tennessee to North Carolina, from Virginia to Maryland, the Vagabonds acted more like kids at camp than men on vacation.

Edison rested on riverbanks and led campfire chats.

Ford flipped flapjacks and toppled trees.

Burroughs hiked the hills and penned poems.

And Firestone—well, he was game for anything!

Their camping experiment was so much fun, the
faithful friends planned another trip the
following summer.

This time, the friends packed their tents and headed
for the back roads of New England. Their road trips
got the two inventors thinking . . . and tinkering!
Why not make camping a little easier?

With the power from his batteries,
EDISON, THE WIZARD OF MENLO PARK,
TURNED THEIR MOONLESS CAMPSITE INTO A WELL-LIT STAGE!

And with the addition of a refrigerator, stove, and a sink,
FORD, THE TIN LIZZIE TITAN,
TURNED A TRUCK INTO A KITCHEN ON WHEELS!

Thanks to Edison's home movies, folks packed
theaters to see the famous four roughing it.
Now everyone wanted to join the fun!

With each passing mile on each summer journey,
curious crowds grew larger and larger.

From farm fields and city streets, folks rushed
to meet the men who had changed their lives.

Gone were the campers' carefree days and peaceful nights. The Vagabonds' vacations were starting to feel a lot like **WORK!**

"All good things...

...must come to an end."

"Remember that time with the crocodile?

After years of back-road summer escapes,
the famous friends finally packed away their tents.
Although their road trips came to a halt,
their friendships traveled on.

Thanks to the inventors' frolicking fun adventures, folks all across America—families and not-so-famous friends—started cranking up their own Model Ts, ready to escape their busy lives, and invent camping adventures of their own . . .

ROAD TRIPS!

YOSEMITE

BIG BEND

AFTERWORD

Edison, Burroughs, Ford, and Firestone on Old Evans Mill waterwheel in West Virginia, 1918

Thomas Edison, Henry Ford, Harvey Firestone, and John Burroughs enjoyed many summer camping trips together between 1914 and 1924. The Four Vagabonds, as they called themselves, seemed an unlikely team. The ages of the four famous friends spanned over forty years, but their simple childhoods, insatiable curiosity, and love of nature bound them together as loyal friends and traveling companions.

While the manufacturing pioneers, Edison, Ford, and Firestone, were three of the wealthiest men in America, Burroughs lived a simple, Spartan life in the rustic woods of upstate New York. Thanks to the naturalist's best-selling books, Burroughs had thousands of fans of his own.

Before 1913, when Ford's assembly line created the Model T—the first car affordable for nearly every American—the only people pitching tents and sleeping under the stars were typically in the army or without a home. Once Ford established the forty-hour workweek and the five-dollar daily wage for his workers, more and more Americans had the money to buy Ford cars and the time to take recreational road trips of their own.

The Vagabonds' summer trips became grander productions each year. In 1919, the camping caravan grew to fifty vehicles filled with supplies, food, cooks, and staff—along with a few lucky friends and family members. The inventors who brought the future inside people's homes found ways to take it outside as well. Ford designed two of the trucks to supply their campsites with a full working kitchen and storage for their foldable furniture, forerunners of today's recreational vehicles, or RVs. The round, folding, dining table with a lazy Susan in the middle seated twenty. Edison's battery gave the campers, and the world, electric lights on a string. The creators of the world's first affordable cars, rubber tires, electric lights, batteries, and motion-picture cameras, along with an expert naturalist, made the perfect team for introducing the world to recreational camping.

Henry Ford, the self-appointed camp director, organized competitions for the Vagabonds—no doubt staged for reporters and photographers. Out in the wilds they ran races, shot targets, cradled wheat, and chopped or climbed trees. When forced into hotels due to bad weather or car trouble, Ford invented indoor contests. At the age of seventy-one, Thomas Edison won the high-kicking contest by kicking a cigar off the edge of a fireplace mantel, not once, not twice, but three times in a row! Burroughs won the title of champion tree chopper—beating Ford by only a second. Henry Ford bested his friends by hopping up ten stairs in only two hops. And Harvey Firestone was declared the wheat-cradling contest champion by the judge, Thomas Edison.

The Vagabonds' camping adventures became so popular even President Warren Harding joined in during the summer of 1921. The photographs and articles in newspapers and Edison's home movies shown in theaters across the country brought more reporters, photographers, and admirers along on the camping trips.

Burroughs joined his friends for his last trip in 1920 when he was eighty-three. The remaining Vagabonds took their last road trip together in 1924, when the growing crowds made it impossible for them to enjoy the peace and quiet they had originally set out to find. Thanks to the publicity the famous camping adventures gathered, support grew for increased access and development of public parks and forests across the country. The inventors' camping experiment inspired millions to discover America's natural treasures by way of a new favorite pastime—recreational camping.

Edison, Burroughs, and Ford at Edison's winter home in Fort Myers, Florida, in 1914. Ford buys the estate next door two years later. The "friendship gate" between their Winter Estates (now a museum) always remained open.

Edison enjoys a nap at a Maryland campsite in 1921, while President Harding reads a newspaper beside Harvey Firestone.

Firestone and Ford peel potatoes with a camp chef on the 1921 camping trip.

During the week of July 21–27, 1921, President Warren Harding (middle, reading paper) joined Ford, Edison (front left), and Firestone (front far right) on their first camping trip after John Burroughs died earlier that year. It was also the first time their wives joined the Vagabond campers. A plaque now memorializes their historic visit inside the Camp Harding County Park, Big Pool, Maryland.

Thomas Edison—the inventor of the phonograph, the incandescent lightbulb, the alkaline battery, and scores of other inventions that earned him 1,093 U.S. patents— relaxes on a camping chair.

Always one to keep busy, Henry Ford chops wood at their Maryland campsite in 1921. One of Ford's favorite quotes was, "Chop your own wood, and it will warm you twice."

THE VAGABONDS ON THEIR FELLOW VAGABONDS

Burroughs, Edison, and Ford pose in front of one of their Ford camping cars.

HENRY FORD ON JOHN BURROUGHS

"He declared that the automobile was going to kill the appreciation of nature. . . . I thought that his emotions had taken him on the wrong tack and so I sent him an automobile with the request that he try it out and discover for himself whether it would not help him to know nature better. That automobile . . . completely changed his point of view. He found that it helped him to see more.

Out of that automobile grew our friendship, and it was a fine one. No man could help being the better for knowing John Burroughs."

HARVEY FIRESTONE ON THOMAS EDISON

"He reads a great deal and he remembers what he reads, so that he can talk deeply on any subject. As everyone knows, he is an indomitable worker, but when he is on vacation he does not try to work. He does exactly what he pleases: he goes to bed late and rises late, and whenever there is nothing else to do, he either goes to sleep or reads a newspaper. He is lost without a newspaper!"

JOHN BURROUGHS

"[Edison] is cushiony and adjustable, and always carries his own shock absorbers with him."

"Partly owing to his more advanced age, but mainly, no doubt, to his more meditative and introspective cast of mind, he is far less active than is Mr. Ford. When we would pause for the mid-day lunch, or to make camp at the end of the day, Mr. Edison would sit in his car and read, or curl up, boy fashion, under a tree and take a nap, while Mr. Ford would inspect the stream or busy himself in getting wood for the fire. Mr. Ford is a runner and a high kicker, and frequently challenged some of the party to race with him. He is also a persistent walker, and from every camp, both morning and evening, he sallied forth for a brisk half-hour walk."

"Mr. Firestone belongs to an entirely different type—the clean, clear-headed, conscientious business type, always on his job, always ready for whatever comes, always at the service of those around him, devoted to his family and his friends, sound in his ideas, and generous of the wealth that has come to him as a manufacturer."

FUNNY VAGABOND CAMPING STORIES

John Burroughs (1837–1921)

SECRET SANTA

"Abraham Lincoln 'Link' Sines, a Maryland State Forest warden, introducing the famous campers to a hardware store owner, Mr. Naylor:

'Mr. Naylor, I'd like to introduce you to Thomas Edison; he invented that light bulb on your ceiling. This is Henry Ford; he manufactured your car parked outside your store; and this is Mr. Firestone; he made the tires that are on your car.'

Mr. Naylor then looked at Burroughs and said, 'And I suppose you're going to tell me that this man with the beard is Santa Claus!'"

MUDDILY AMUSED

"The campers didn't drive only Fords on their trips . . .

When Ford's Lincoln got stuck in the mud, a neighboring boy watched a horse pull it out and said to Henry Ford: 'Mister, you have the wrong kind of car. My father drives a Ford and it never gets stuck in the mud.' Amused by the boy's response, Ford asked for the name and address of his father and had a brand new Ford delivered to their home."

AFFORD A FORD

"A salesman, presumably on his way to make a call in the next town, experienced an auto breakdown that drew Ford's attention. With screwdriver and pliers, he fixed the problem and soon had the anxious man ready to move on again. The man insisted on paying for the service, unaware of the identity of his famous repairman. Ford declined, saying something to the effect that he had enough money to last him many life times. Skeptically, the man replied that Ford could not be very rich or he would not be riding in a Ford car!"

Seated around their collapsible table in 1921: Mrs. Edison and her husband to the left of the center pole; President Harding, Mrs. Firestone, and Henry Ford to the right of the pole.

BURROUGHS WROTE

"It was here [Bolar Springs, Virginia] that Mr. Edison gave several children standing about a nickel each. When asked if they knew his name, a little girl answered, 'Yes, Mr. Gramophone.'"

SELECTED BIBLIOGRAPHY

All quotations used in the book can be found in the following sources marked with an asterisk (*).

* Brauer, Norman. *There to Breathe the Beauty*. Dalton, PA: Norman Brauer Publications, 1995.

* Burroughs, John. Letter to Thomas Edison and Harvey Firestone, December 11, 1916.

* ———. *Our Vacation Days of 1918*. Privately printed by Harvey Firestone, 1918.

* ———. "A Strenuous Holiday." In *Under the Maples*. Boston and New York: Houghton Mifflin, 1921.

Burroughs, John, Thomas Edison, and Harvey Firestone. *In Nature's Laboratory: Commemorating Our Vacation Trip of 1916, August 28th to September 9th* (privately published).

* Burroughs, John, and Clifton Johnson. *John Burroughs Talks: His Reminiscences and Comments*. Boston and New York: Houghton Mifflin, 1922.

Ford, Henry, with Samuel Crowther. *Edison as I Know Him*. New York: Cosmopolitan Book Corporation, 1930.

* ———. *My Life and Work*. Garden City, NY: Doubleday, Page & Company, 1922.

Newton, James D. *Uncommon Friends: Life with Thomas Edison, Henry Ford, Harvey Firestone, Alexis Carrel, and Charles Lindbergh*. Orlando, FL: Harcourt Brace Jovanovich, 1989.

Renehan, Edward. *John Burroughs: An American Naturalist*. Hensonville, NY: Black Dome Press, 1998.

Sorensen, Charles E., with Samuel T. Williamson. *My Forty Years with Ford*. New York: W. W. Norton, 1956.

Twitchell, James B. *Winnebago Nation: The RV in American Culture*. New York: Columbia University Press, 2014.

Watts, Steven. *The People's Tycoon: Henry Ford and the American Century*. New York: Vintage, 2006.

RELATED CHILDREN'S BOOKS

Barretta, Gene. *Timeless Thomas: How Thomas Edison Changed Our Lives*. New York: Square Fish/Henry Holt, 2017.

Brown, Don. *A Wizard from the Start: The Incredible Boyhood and Amazing Inventions of Thomas Edison*. Boston: Houghton Mifflin Books for Children, 2010.

Burgan, Michael. *Who Was Henry Ford?* New York: Grosset & Dunlap, 2014.

Frith, Margaret. *Who Was Thomas Alva Edison?* New York: Grosset & Dunlap, 2005.

Slade, Suzanne. *The Inventor's Secret: What Thomas Edison Told Henry Ford*. Watertown, MA: Charlesbridge, 2015.

Thomas, Peggy. *Full of Beans: Henry Ford Grows a Car*. New York: Calkins Creek, 2019.

DVDS, VIDEO LINKS, DIGITAL COLLECTIONS, AND ONLINE SOURCES

Websites active at time of publication

* Burroughs, John. *Our Vacation Days of 1918*. Privately printed by Harvey Firestone, 1918. The Henry Ford, Collections and Research, Digital Collections. thehenryford.org/collections-and-research/digital-collections/artifact/376639#slide=gs-264885.

* ———. "A Strenuous Holiday." In *Under the Maples*. Boston and New York: Houghton Mifflin, 1921. Internet Archive. archive.org/stream/undermaples00burr#page/108/mode/2up.

* Burroughs, John, and Clifton Johnson. *John Burroughs Talks: His Reminiscences and Comments*. Boston and New York: Houghton Mifflin, 1922. Internet Archive. archive.org/stream/cu31924021985522#page/n0/mode/2up.

"Camping in Nature's Laboratory with Thomas Edison." Thomas Edison National Historic Park, National Park Service. Online exhibit of photographs, telegrams, letters, and videos, Google Arts & Culture. artsandculture.google.com/exhibit/IAJyi-hAK4E9Lw.

* Ford, Henry, with Samuel Crowther. *My Life and Work*. Garden City, NY: Doubleday, Page & Company, 1922. Internet Archive. archive.org/details/mylifework01ford.

"Henry Ford 'Camping' with Edison and Firestone." *American Experience*. PBS, January 29, 2013. pbs.org/video/american-experience-henry-ford-camping-edison-and-firestone.

"Into the Wild: Edison, Ford and Friends." *WGCU Presents*. WGCU, April 11, 2011. video.wgcu.org/video/wgcu-presents-into-the-wild-edison-ford-friends.

Lewis, Dr. David L. "The Illustrious Vagabonds." Henry Ford Heritage Association. hfha.org/the-ford-story/the-illustrious-vagabonds.

Wianecki, Shannon. "When America's Titans of Industry and Innovation Went Road-Tripping Together." *Smithsonian*, January 26, 2016. smithsonianmag.com/history/when-americas-titans-industry-and-innovation-went-road-tripping-together-180957924.

Zumbrun, Francis Champ. "Famous Travelers: Edison, Ford, Firestone." Maryland Department of Natural Resources (no date). Originally Published in *Cumberland Times News*, November 1, 2008. dnr.maryland.gov/Pages/md-conservation-history/travelers.aspx.

* ———. "Famous Travelers: Edison, Ford, Firestone; A Memorial Service Is Held for John Burroughs at Camp Harding." Maryland Department of Natural Resources. dnr.maryland.gov/Pages/md-conservation-history/TravelersPart3.aspx.

———. "Famous Travelers: Edison, Ford, Firestone; Promote Outdoor Recreation with a President." Maryland Department of Natural Resources. dnr.maryland.gov/Pages/md-conservation-history/TravelersPart2.aspx.

* ———. "Famous Travelers: Edison, Ford, Firestone; Travel through Allegany County." Maryland Department of Natural Resources. dnr.maryland.gov/Pages/md-conservation-history/TravelersPart1.aspx.

* ———. "Famous Travelers: Edison, Ford, Firestone; The Vagabonds Camp at Muddy Creek Falls." Maryland Department of Natural Resources. dnr.maryland.gov/Pages/md-conservation-history/TravelersPart5.aspx.

* ———. "Famous Travelers: Edison, Ford, Firestone; Vagabonds Remembered for Work, but Loved Nature." Maryland Department of Natural Resources. dnr.maryland.gov/Pages/md-conservation-history/TravelersPart7.aspx.

MUSEUMS AND HISTORICAL SITES

Edison and Ford Winter Estates
2350 McGregor Boulevard
Fort Myers, Florida 33901
(239) 334-7419
edisonfordwinterestates.org

Greenfield Village (Henry Ford Museum)
Dearborn, Michigan 48124
(313) 982-6001
thehenryford.org/visit/greenfield-village

The Henry Ford Museum of American Innovation
20900 Oakwood Boulevard
Dearborn, Michigan 48124
(313) 982-6001
thehenryford.org/visit/henry-ford-museum

John Burroughs Nature Sanctuary and Slabsides
261 Floyd Ackert Road
West Park, New York 12493
(845) 384-6320
johnburroughsassociation.org

The Thomas Edison Center at Menlo Park
37 Christie Street
Edison, New Jersey 08820
(732) 549-3299
menloparkmuseum.org

Thomas Edison National Historical Park:
211 Main Street
West Orange, New Jersey 07052
(973) 736-0550, ext. 11
nps.gov/edis/index.htm

ACKNOWLEDGMENTS

Sincere thanks to the reading-room staff at the Benson Ford Research Center; Brent Newman and Matt Andres, curators at the Edison and Ford Winter Estates; the amazing folks at the Highlights Foundation; and special thanks to my navigators, Carolyn Yoder and Rachel Orr.

PICTURE CREDITS

Edison and Ford Winter Estates: 34 (top); 36;
Everett Collection Inc / Alamy Stock Photo: 34 (center);
Library of Congress, Prints and Photographs Division,
LC-DIG-ds-00555: 34 (bottom); LC-DIG-hec-31266: 35 (top);
LC-DIG-hec-31279: 35 (center); LC-DIG-hec-31270:
35 (bottom); LC-USZ62-86843: 37 (top); LC-DIG-hec-31273:
37 (bottom); Pictorial Press Ltd / Alamy Stock Photo: 32;
Jodie Otte: author photo: cover (back flap top);
Paris Dilorenzo: illustrator photo: cover (back flap bottom).

For Winn, my favorite road-tripping companion —CF

For Jennifer, Paxton, Charlie, Paris, and Tim —JH

Calkins Creek
An imprint of Astra Books for Young Readers,
a division of Astra Publishing House
astrapublishinghouse.com
Printed in China

ISBN: 978-1-68437-272-0 (hc)
ISBN: 978-1-63592-461-9 (eBook)
Library of Congress Control Number: 2021918213

First edition
10 9 8 7 6 5 4 3 2 1

Design by Barbara Grzeslo
The text is set in Pitch Sans Semi Bold and
Times New Roman.
The titles are set in Roper.
The art for *Road Trip!* was created using cut paper,
watercolor, and pastels. The individual pieces of
cut paper were hand-rendered, glued,
and assembled into the final illustrations.